THE Music

Authenticity Code

By SheisL1, the artist

Leigh Hickombottom, the person

The information in this book is intended to be educational and informative based off of SheisL1's real life.

Book design photo by and © Leigh P. Hickombottom/ SheisL1

For more information please visit www.TheMusicSheisL1.com

ISBN (Paperback) 978-0-9914529-6-5

ISBN (e-Book) 978-0-9914529-8-9

Dedication

In honor of my children, whom I wish to choose and pave their own paths, not according to outside people but instead according to their true North. According to their own greatness that they should through themselves, not through watching others live vicariously. Place none above you. Love you. Because I do. Dream big and know you can and will achieve your dream accomplished and actualized.

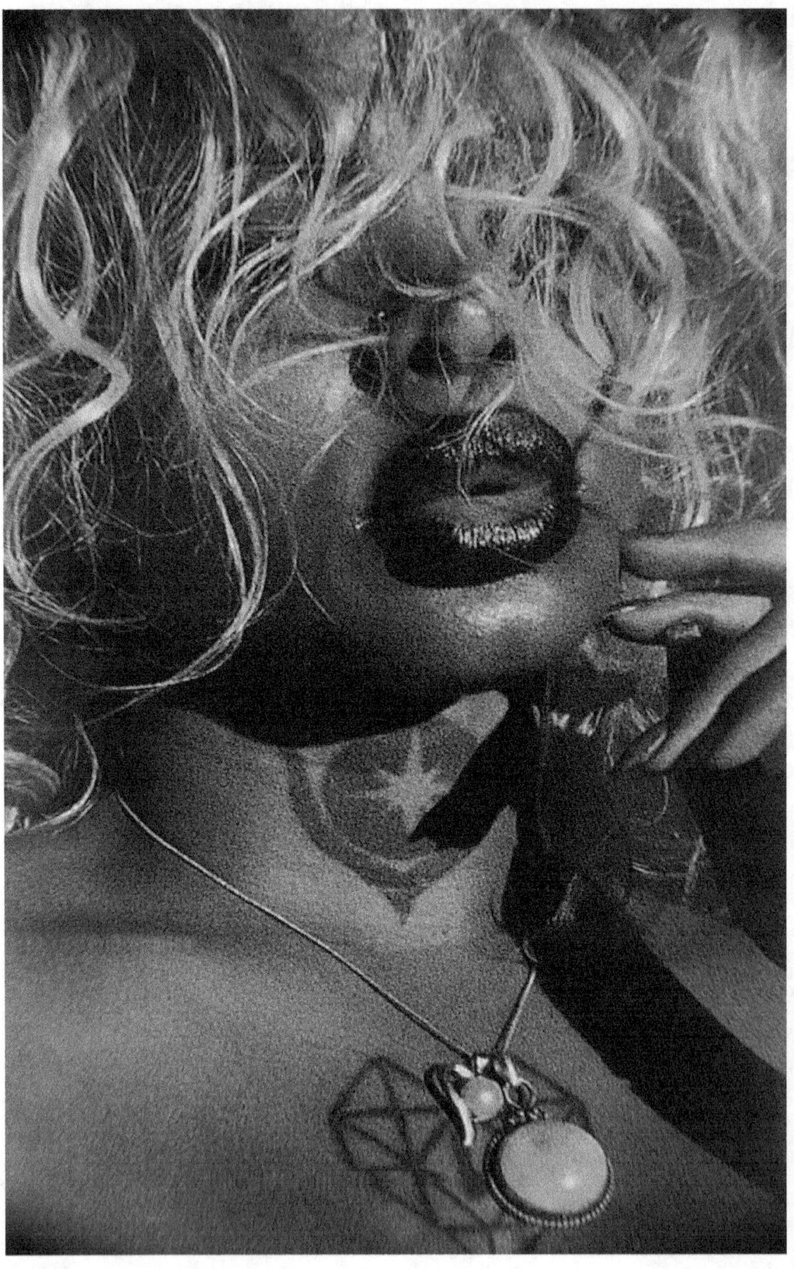

Note:

I said this in my previous books, *The Music*, The Music: Loveology X Integrity and this still holds true. If you are reading this, it is because you want something more, something real you can feel and you aspire real growth. So let's grow. Again, this third booklet is written with my truth. Keep that in mind for your journey.

This third book is about staying on your journey according to you and living your truth and your truth alone.

Though experiences and people may try to push you off track or try to change your course to accord with something or someone you are not and that does not have at heart your best interest or TRUEVISION long-term, stay true to your inner code and self. You know who you are. Sometimes others just know who they want you to be. Then there are others that know who you can become while staying true to yourself. Knowing the difference is everything in a true connection and in real life.

It is not the things that are force-fed to us that impact us profoundly. At least not for a group of us: those others like me that I know exist. Stay strong. Trust your intuition. Pay attention to who and what you allow to connect with you and your truth. Those meant to stay will, if nothing else have some if not all of these major qualities:

1. They have your best interest in mind along with theirs of course (We mind).

2. They are reading the same book, so to speak, if not being on the same page, and that's okay.

3. They are open-minded enough to see your uniqueness and embrace it instead of trying to mold it into outdated forms and something you are not.

4. They will respect your personal boundaries, and hopefully you will do the same for them.

5. They will help you push through your creative boundaries/limitations and nurture your gifts.

6. They will keep it 1,000% real not 100% and nothing less because they respect themselves and would want the same. The bar must be raised. This comes from me both observing and experiencing situations in my own experiences.

7. They choose you and accept you as you truly are.

Keep these people close and do the same for them. These are your true people. Stand up for them. Stand up *with* them. This allows acceptance of genuine artistry.

Table of Contents

Open the booklet to a random page and get the message for you in the moment. Then Read from the beginning. Be inspired to read without paying attention to time or the page numbers. You can do it!!

Where am I now since my last book, "*The Music: Loveology X Integrity*".

Whelp, I'm still on my journey. That's for sure. I am still in a place of gratitude for the work and growth I have been able to experience. I've learned a lot more about me and why I choose what I choose as well as why it is so important to for me to stick to my truths and inner wisdom. Creating is what I have been doing and will continue to do but not for the perspective of another. Others have their voices, should they choose. I choose my voice and perspective and no one's scales but my own.

I have created a lot. I have stepped away at times from my own intuition and came right back because my inner wisdom knows who and what is best for me at any given time. So does yours, by the way, if you tap inward instead of checking outward first. The easiest way I have found for someone to get lost is when they value more highly what is outside of them, and what the outside is saying is good for them as an individual, rather than valuing, listening to the individual they are.

On my journey, there seem to still be many comparisons being made: people wanting artists to be like the artist before rather than honoring the uniqueness that an individual artist brings forth for all our betterment and honoring them that way. Collaborating with them instead of trying to mold them into someone before them seems like the win, in my mind anyway. So, while that is still going on to date, I have also been creating according to who I AM. I am grateful for that freedom.

If you are creating, you have also noticed some changes in the music world too. I hope it keeps getting better. Like honoring the root but being open to the (as I've said in the past) much-needed future ahead. Those are the unique voices, artists in expression of all walks of life, who can feel and are appreciated and acknowledged as beautiful for being different, and who are honoring the things that unite us instead of trying to fit in.

I have noticed changes in sound and what seems to be "in" at the moment and do like a lot of it. Now I'm always, in a playlist, looking only for those feel-good vibes and unique voices and sounds. When I see they are also doing well on the charts, it makes me happy. Truly. Yes, even some of those mainstream songs I've noticed incorporating some awesomeness juice into their new sounds, songs, and even productions. I love that.

Prospering together, truly supporting one another because it feels right by nature is accurate to my design. I honestly still feel like a lone wolf. That part sucks. You know, waiting for the true soul family to show up and stand by your side so you can cheer them on and they can do the same, physically. At the same time, life and cocreating is rewarding still because I am still creating and staying true to my design on my time, even with attempts of interferences. What feels good to me intuitively matters and takes precedence in my works and cocreations. It is not what and who I am told should feel or be good for me that matters.

As far as right in this moment, I'm visiting my favorite café in Orlando and writing this for you. I released a new EP titled *More Life and updated to current time, I have also just released Love Me Right Ep at the end of December.* Autumn just started and those beautiful fall colors I love are peeking through in nature and into the chill, ambient sound that went into cocreating this album. The album More Life has six tracks, with Love me right having five tracks. All of these I will get into a little later. I love these works like all of the creations the universe allows itself to flow through this vessel, unique to who I AM. I am very grateful. I'm almost always amazed by the finished product of these cocreations and the fact that I am still able to create according to who I AM uniquely according to my vibe at the moment and purpose.

I've learned a lot more about me, but not necessarily anything I did not know. Awakening to learning new things about me has helped me embrace ALL of me, and at the beginning and end of each day, that is what matters to me. Do I like what I see and what I have created, not just in art but in life? Most times, the answer is yes. Some days the answer is that I can do better by my own scales, so I try to fix it and do better. I hope we all do. Each person's journey is and absolutely should be their own, and my wish for you is that you move, create, and live according to you and what and who you believe in. Believe in you first. That's something I would have told my younger self. Don't place yourself lower than another. There are different paths, yes, but they will all eventually lead to the same road. Trust that.

I am still in a place where I believe that we as artists, as people, as cocreators must believe in a higher power or something greater than ourselves that is connected to ourselves as ONE. What that means and what that looks like and who all that is, is for you to decide. Know so strongly that the foundation cannot break but instead expand and shift to allow in more. More life. More love. More growth. Believe in something that empowers you. Fear is not that.

I truly know that what you choose to empower or connect with is important. The who, what, and where are important to growth. Choose these things as (hopefully) wisely as you choose the water you drink, the food you intake. These things have just as much of an impact on your vessel and your creativity. Don't be bound. Be loving and connected to what nourishes who you truly are. That is you, raw and for real. Since writing the last book, I've had an opportunity to test this out myself. Nourishment. We all need it, as do your family, your peers, and kindred souls.

Since my last book, I wouldn't say I have strayed away; however, my focus on certain things that I truly value, love, and that have real meaning for me, that are beyond priceless, has not received as much nourishment, love, and protection as the things, people, connections that I did and did not allow to distract me and use up my precious time and energy. Things done against my will and my wheel. That is not a good feeling. Not a good feeling at all. So I am still at the moment looking for things to get back on track according to my true design and life's mission, while waiting on the universe to step in with all its resources as cocreator as it has always been and bring time and wheel correct. Time, like my energy, your energy, our energy, is priceless, and I cannot emphasize this enough.

The creative you needs you, needs us, to make it count. This means meaningful, prolific, profound seconds, moments, days, years. What I'm saying is Time itself. Art itself depends on it in order to authentically create and shift, as does life according to true design. You are genuinely needed to be the art in order to authentically create and shift. That is a profound epiphany, so sit, breathe, and let that resonate with your soul and who you are. Right where you are in this moment, as you are in this moment.

The true essence of you

The true essence of you will not be found as bits and pieces of others. If the mirror is correct and clean it should reflect who you are, not you as another person. Remember your journey is yours and theirs is theirs. Have you taken the time to sit within yourself, to notice when something is not true or correct in your daily reflections? You should know yourself better than anyone else. You should know yourself inside and out. There should be no false concept allowed to steer you from the truth of who you are and who you are meant to be. That's all of you in complete totality.

We should know and learn as much about ourselves as possible so that we are able to use that awesomeness to create. With learning about who we are in essence and physical truth, we should embrace it all. Knowing allows you to understand your value so that you accept nothing less and do not allow the lowering of your value to appease another. They say you can't love if you don't love yourself. That, in my experience, is a half-truth. I've watched people pour out love firsthand to others while placing themselves second. Not because they didn't love themselves but because they were being selfless. They knew they were a vessel that should never stop overflowing with love. So, they gave. Even to those that didn't deserve.

So, yes, you can give certain things that are and should be free, such as love, while not receiving it fully back. However, this does not mean you do not love yourself in all cases. When I say this I need you to understand as I have written in print before. Love is multifaceted. There are different forms of love from universal, family, a mother to a child, a romantic relationship, friendships and more. Some forms are unconditional and some are not.

The essence of you. What is the essence of you? Have you taken the time to go inward and discover? It is not enough to know that you have similarities with others. You are meant and deserve to be different and unique. Your essence should thrive. Your physical self should thrive. Your works should thrive. Know who you are. Love you in your way. Just make sure your love of you is unconditional.

The journey so far: Hard or easy

Depends on what part of this journey we are talking about.

Creating is a gift given to me from the universe at birth. The ability and true skill to be able to create, that is. I think we are all gifted to create in some form or fashion. We are always creating/cocreating. That skill and ability has been about the same for me. Now, if you ask a couple of other questions, like have you had to deal with obstacles, or with more of people's projections and with attempted delays to throw you off course, or normal or not-so-normal things artists go through… Whelp…

I feel there have been more attempts to throw obstacles and projections, beyond tests and interferences, to get me to not follow my true heart, true dreams, and to continue doing what I've done in many ways through many outlets since I was young. You know being the real me, creatively. As resent as January the 15th 2023, Still dealing with people who have tried to continue to mess and manipulate my time and interfere with what I am destined for. That sucks and has truly been disheartening; it has intuitively proved me right in my precious thoughts of the whos (etc.) that were and were not in my best interest, genuinely, as a person, mother, sister, ally, and true artist. Real. But in saying this, know that this adversity does not stop me by any means from having and pursuing my TRUE dreams and goals with the people who matter the most, regardless of the attempts to keep me from those I love and the artistic gifts with which I was born.

In this regard, I say, keep following your dream, trusting your intuition, knowing who you are and accepting all of who you are for the sake of your heart, soul, and leaving your TRUE Signature in and on this world. You are priceless and when you know your gifts and who you are, that is priceless too. You deserve to financially prosper off of your life, your ideas, your gifts in excellence and good form. Anything less is an insult to true, genuine artistry authentic. It is an insult to the creative mind, heart, and true soul. Especially those artists who pull from other artists without giving acknowledgement and pay or gaining permission first. At least to me and other deserving artists who are different but like myself, independently having to do it all almost on my own without an entourage of people doing the work for me creatively and intuitively. Because that's the way I create true to Leigh Hickombottom design.

With that said, I have cocreated physically with others as of the present, with the use of apps and such to help along the way. For this I am grateful, but I miss the sometimes much-needed physical human connection of having people who have an open mind to your vision (not to harm or tear it apart but to help and cocreate with you for the benefit of we, us, and the world alike). Not only for us but people also like me. Like us.

We must be reading the same book. Maybe not the same page, but working in the best genuine interest of one another. Being able to openly be vulnerable and honest enough as souls, as artists, enough to respectfully cocreate together and create something beautiful. We must be able to be honest and real for real while honoring what you each consider artistry according to the real you.

This coming from a socially selective and by nature hermetic person. I feel that this aspect, for those like myself, may be a little harder, but I know when the blessings, gifts, real acknowledgement for our works become actualized it will be well worth it. Our hard work. By no one else's standards but our own. I say this because I feel standards are subjective and depending. Depending on what, you might ask? For starters, we all know that what is easy to one may be hard to another. So, I say subjective, as in, if you have worked internally to master yourself for your art, yourself, and your authentic artistry true and authentic for a month, a year, or even ten years, and you have physically put in that inner work, you know that it is a beast in itself and requires much more than beyond the eyes (or meets the eyes), both physically and mentally. It's not easy at all and everyone doesn't actually want to improve themselves.

Now, you might be the artist or person who put in physical work, busting your butt and working hard in performances, shows, etc. You know that requires a whole lot too, both physically and mentally, but in a different way. Both demand respect in their respective ways.

Yes, from my true perspective, working on me, my mind, heart, and soul to get them re-aligned with who I know myself to be in being, as an artist, and person multidimensionally and all-encompassing true, yes. It's been a bit—not so much hard as a shock—to see things I've worked hard for, based off of the genuine person that I am with the good intentions that I have for certain things, being thrown off purposefully and purposely misused through vessels and voices I would not choose , nor grant permission.

I feel everyone goes through experiences on whatever path they are on in reaching both their personal and career goals and trying to maintain them. Don't give up! Don't give up! And be true to who you are so that you can live your dream and not watch it lived through others. Especially those gifts that were meant for you that were specifically designed by the universe for your vessel to express in only the way you authentically can. It's easy to get discouraged, but it's so rewarding to finish and follow through.

We all are destined for greatness in special ways. While I have not yet had the ability to fully experience what I know I was created for, destined for, I am truly grateful for the journey thus far and being able to walk my path according to who I AM. I can't wait to write a book and tell you how my own personal hard work has paid off to give you hope to be you and okay with who you are as an artist and as a person.

So, back to has the journey been harder or easier. Answered. Most important is that the journey has been self-rewarding to me, soulfully as a creative being. I am still doing what I TRULY LOVE. I am still doing what I truly love as a creative being in my way. So, anything that has come up to attempt to make me change my mind, throw me off course, or interfere has not deterred me. All of what has incurred makes me know even more how important what I am doing is and why it must be done. It makes me want it more but with all the other gifts I came into this world with to express distinctively, uniquely, and truly through this vessel as it was and is. I AM supposed to be writing this right now. So I AM.

Let go of, hold on to

Well, let's go. First, let go of placing someone above you. I've said this before in past books and will say it again because it is so very important that I wish as a child my parents had told me this. Or that I'd thought in such a way to remind me of this myself. I have told my own children not to compare themselves to others, wishing that they would never place another above themselves in their own minds. That's powerful. Admire and appreciate but never wish or want to be anything other than who you are. You are beautiful—flaws, quirks, and all. Your team, people, and family will know this and inspire you to both embrace this truth and shine because of it.

Second, I would say, let go of needing mostly outside validation. We each have people whose thoughts about our works or creations we value. But we must first value our creations ourselves and be unmoved in what others feel is right for your vision. There are a couple of exceptions here. Cocreating with someone being one of them. But at the end of the day, it's your name attached to it. Are you proud? Do you like it?

Third, let go of people who do not have your best interest at heart and who interfere with your true happiness, which for me is my children and creating art. Your group of people will support you and your dreams. I've learned to fully release and let go of those who have interfered with things such as my genuine love of my children and I being together and creating as I was born to do and as my children were born to do their way true to original blueprint.

Fourth, let go of doubting your own power and greatness. Don’t give it away. It was meant to be utilized through you. If you were blessed (and I say blessed because that is what it is) with a gift, talent, or idea, there is a reason for it. Let go and give it your all. In your way.

Fifth and finally, let go of whatever you feel holds you back from living your dreams and instead live your dreams vividly with your true people and family.

The Value of you

It is so important that you learn and know who you are without being attached to someone else's journey. Your journey was already designed for you with free will movement and choices in place to help you reach your goals. Again, although you admire people you see in the lime light, do not by any means place them above you based of what you see, hear or read and what is specifically placed out there for you to see. They say everything is not what it seems and in my experience that is true.

Try to take the time to go inside yourself first and tap into your inner light and truth. You will find information is displayed differently this way. In the process you will hopefully learn all of your beautiful gift you have to learn and hone in on. Whatever you believe in, God, Source, angels, guides etc. will help you on your mission/assignment to learn and be you authentically connected as one but unique to you. Your unique creations might be inspired by someone or something but you will not try and pretend to be them personified (unless permissioned and paid). It will not pulled from another not without permission from them and their higher self. It will be a gift. Creating and even cocreating is not stealing. So do not misuse the mind of another, the gifts of another.

It is so important to move music and the world ford in correct design. What I've seen is some attempts by some. And few have the right idea but it is still missing major components to the equation and they cannot get that through pretending. The intuitive group that all my booklets were written for are somewhat of what some might call starseeds and or just plain intuitive. But this group is here to cause and bring about great commotion for the betterment of this world and Hu-Man-kind. They are wanting and need the future sound and vibration forward and I cannot wait to truly see that design correct and moved in the right direction with specifically the correct people not misrepresenting a whole future's correct design.

Value yourself. Anyone who is legit and comfortable with who they are when they truly takes a look into the mirror with clear conscious will tell you not to be anyone other than yourself because that's what this world needs to thrive. I'm saying be real, be true and let you shine while appreciating another person's journey. That's why it's imperative to have a code such as authenticity code for your real life regardless of chosen career and life's path.

Authenticity code

Honestly, the best way to start is by going within. You know your inner compass on what respectfully feels right with integrity. You have a basic knowledge of just plain right and wrong in daily life because this shows in artist etiquette.

1. Be true to who you are.

Read this repeatedly for positive reinforcement. You as an artist understand the importance of being true to who you are and your artistry through your creations and your true journey. Tap in inside to make sure you are following your true North. If it feels right, then keep on point. If it doesn't, then adjust until it suits you, not outsiders, and adjust during the process. Feeling and being true is one of the biggest rewards in and of itself. It has to feel right and true to *you* first of all. At least to me, as a unique individual, this means the world.

2. Be your word.

All right, so it doesn't matter what kind of artist you are, just be your word. Do what you say you will do even if it takes time. Just do it. It is much more respectable and its part of your individual energetic signature. Surround yourself with like-minded people and artists, show up, follow through, and keep your word. Your people will support you.

3. Keep your promises. Back to keeping your word, keep your promise. If you are collaborating with others and make a promise/give your word, keep it. It is as simple as that, in action. I feel if the intention is legitimate, with true intent we can and should get it done. I know I want people to keep their promises. So, let's do the same for them.

4. Respect yourself enough to respect others and your and their boundaries. Place boundaries and make sure you and others adhere to them. The beautiful thing about creatively working with other artists like yourself, and even artists on the other side of the spectrum from you, is that you get to learn and share ideas to create something beautiful and hopefully fulfilling. So, respect who they are and their creative boundaries as you would want your own respect.

Codes for me as an artist

Primarily, this is what is important to me as a person and artist in one.

Authenticity

Own who you are. Move and create accordingly. Develop and follow your own code. Mine is just a guideline, as should that of anyone you read or hear about. Authenticity is truly beautiful. As in art, as in life. Those who support you should want you to thrive as the person you are while doing or creating your artistry. Not to say they won't want to see you grow, learn more, and even try more. But they wouldn't want you to be someone you're not. Unless your artistry is acting or something.

Vibes

Start with the vibe of something. In a project, I see how it feels and if I am physically cocreating with someone, how our vibes flow together. Like most things I do, the vibes have to feel right. True. So, whatever I am creating it has to be true to the project and feel right to me as an artist authentically. All of my works prove this.

Intuition

Although checking vibes and how something feels is a part of intuition, I feel it's important to intuitively tap in. Tap into your true self. From there, question whether it is authentic to who you are or what you are trying to put out. I pay attention to how something makes me feel and what images, thoughts, symbols, etc. come up while letting a thought of a project marinate. My marinating doesn't usually take that long. Not when I have my usual focused frame of mind, silence and Zen.

Creative Space

Your creative space is very important. Since everything has a vibe, your creative space should be a space that you feel makes you zone in, tap in, and create free-flowingly. Whatever that looks like to you is what it is. For me, that means being connected to the right elements. That could be being in a clean space burning incense, sitting with crystals and dim lights. Better said, ambient lighting to me as a creator. Some days, that can be bright lights. Some days, I need the ocean and sand. Other days, I need to just be near wood or metal or just out in nature as a whole. My mood and what I am trying to cocreate plays a huge factor in how that equation is formulated and what it is. So, whatever gets you in your focused mood and zone, do it. Be it. Breathe it. Wholeheartedly.

Create wholeheartedly (authentically) with intention

What creating whole-heartedly with intention means to me is to create from my heart with intention. That's true emotion when I create. It needs to come from the heart. I need that element (heart) as an artist and as a multidimensional being, as a person. That element alone is the silent sound waves we do not hear that I need and you need too.

Yes, I can create with my mind only, but to have both heart and mind aligned correctly and to create from this space is very powerful for me as an artist and creator. I feel it. I feel and know the difference, as should you in your own artistry. I've tried just the mind alone. And well, yes, it's great. But better than great to me is mind-blowing soul-shifting experiences and creations. To me they are timeless. They are priceless. They are moments of creation and experience we get to share. That I get to share.

Balance

As much as possible, balance. I need quiet time or "me time" to just be. There is balance between creative work, family, and just me time. I have not always had perfect balance like many with creative and family balance at times, but I do try to have them be a part of certain aspects of my creative works. In the end hoping when it's all said and done they understand and it allows them the freedom to learn how to balance that which they love in life as well as knowing the importance of it.

I feel this balance is healthy and everyone needs it. This is not to be confused with being lazy. But even that is okay in moderation from my perspective. For me, that balance might include ocean time, playing in my way of fun, or just reading a book. We all need it. Your creative self appreciates it, I'm sure. I know I do.

Timing

I have work I have put out and some I have not. Based in part on timing. I was asked whether I meet all my deadlines. Usually, yes, I do because I choose my deadlines and make sure I have set time to see that they are met. I try my best to make sure I balance my creative time with my family time. Timing from start to finish matters to me. That means creative time from the start of the project to actually putting it out, delivering the final product.

Guidelines to help keep you on track

The core basis is basically me saying, regardless of what happens on your journey, keep it individualized to who you are. Be inspired by others, but the goal shouldn't be to be like them or even create like them. Tap into who you were born and created to be. No matter what, keep moving forward. Take a break or stand still. Be still but not stagnant. That is a whole different type of energy. Stillness allows you to be in a place of peace to either be reflective, observant, or contemplative.

Stagnation is usually a complacent or even fear-based lack of movement. It is not progressive. It is neither what I consider time efficient nor positive-momentum based. It is a stuck energy that you should not create from unless it is alchemized to create something beautiful to you the artist. Stagnation is definitely not to be confused with downtime. We all need downtime. The balance. The rejuvenation time.

That's just the start! It's part of what comes with being authentic is the basic (but should be a solid foundation) of what I've mentioned before. You being true to you. That does not mean you will not grow, or you cannot act or even create in a certain way. That means whether you choose to create in artistry or entertainment, these choices and paths chosen in life should feel good to you. It should feel true to you. Period.

You will and should try on different hats of who you are, who you aspire to be. By that I mean delve, learn, and try out all the aspects of your creative self. You cannot do that without tapping into you. The different sides of you. Just as there are several emotions, color spectrums and so on, the individualized you also has different facets. You won't know just how beautiful that is if you don't explore you. Get to know you and be true to you. Not the covers of magazines and TV but you, first.

With that said:

*Set your goals, reach those goals your way! I mean that. Yes, I feel that when you choose to cocreate with others, you will have to adjust a few things so your project all flows. But compromise in who you are is not one of these adjustments. Set those goals and make sure you don't miss your mark. Don't set out to try what you have been told is the easiest or hardest way. Try the way that's true to you first. You might find that it will be both hard and easy enough on its own.

*Trust your journey, and if it doesn't look like someone else's, good go for it. Run with it. It was designed to honor your individuality. I am saying this to those like myself who value individuality and recognition for that. There are so many different routes that lead us to our destinations. It is our choice. Be it the one you build and pave with the universe or one already stamped out for you, trust you. The journey was meant to be your own. So, own it, run with it and cherish what is uniquely designed for you, if you let it be. Empower you. Give thanks for those before you and

those who will forge after you, but always choose you. Choose to empower you. That is and can be the beauty of an artistic journey, a life journey being authentic.

*Yes, we are all connected, but you were created to be uniquely connected as one. Image all the beautiful frequencies of life, art, and true beauty you could feel and see with your eyes closed if you choose to live up to your highest self, which is different for everyone. I am specifically talking about those like myself. You choose and then don't let anyone, not even an inner voice, tell you to stop doing or living your purpose. Be the best artist you can be, connected as the correct one.

*Wisdom. We all have the ability to tap into wisdom that we were never really disconnected from and nor should we ever be. Now I don't know if you need this just for artistry or to continue to evolve as a being, a person. But what I do know is that it is so staple to me that I need it as part of my root to thrive as both artist and person. Walk your journey, grow, but whatever you do, do not lose touch or sight and vision of true wisdom. That's inside. Outside can only validate what your soul knows because it is a part of your DNA. Your blueprint.

*Check your work forward and backwards. How does it resonate and vibe with you? I feel at least in my process, it is important to check your work. Depending on what type of artistry you are creating, this should vary. Basically, check every element to a precision point. How does it feel? How does it resonate with you? The color, the sound, the note, the instrument, the canvas, the concept, and so on. Not so much that you should second guess your project, but just to know how your project breathes. How it comes to life. But first, look and feel within to you, forward and backward.

*If you can find like-minded people, great! If not, it's really just a matter of time. Connect with at least open-minded people.

*Never give up. Very self-explanatory. There will be situations, people, experiences and even your own self-doubt or lack of seeing the desired results you know you worked so hard on to make you want to give up. Don't. You will hear and read this from those you admire. I know from some of the artistic people I admire and believe in who are what I consider unique and / or open minded in their own craft (at least from observing): they did not quit. That makes me proud to say keep going too. I can't wait to be standing with them side by side with honor, truth, and the integrity of my own artistry.

*No obstacle is big enough to keep you from living your dreams. Your mind though… Let that big beautiful, magnificent thing be your ally. Make sure you are feeding it the correct nourishment and pay attention to who you allow yourself to connect with and what they feed your mind. There are many ways to use it. Use it to gain wisdom, empower you, and implement correct action on your behalf. Let it cocreate with your heart to lift you up. A masterpiece is made up of multiple ingredients. The mind used correctly is one of them. Open it. Express it. Surpass your own and projected limitations with it, mindfully. Mind fully.

Mind full

Mind full is both in whole and part being mindful. Mindful in creation, intention, and the greatness we are uniquely trying to put out into the world, leaving our own genuine signature. That means the real vibration of you and who you are, who you as a person and artist are meant to become. The greatest you. The highest you, celebrated.

Mindfulness is paying attention to the details. Mindfulness has been and will always be found in the little details. The way you create true to you. The details of your process in creating and following through to the end product or vision. At least this has always been true for me as a cocreator, artist, and multidimensional being, as we all are. Recognize your masterpiece. Be the first to acknowledge it. Be proud. Celebrate it. Be mindful.

Now, in being mindful, I feel we must have the space set in our own mind to feel full with the knowledge, wisdom, and tools to move forward as we were meant to, both in creating our works and thriving in our lives. Part of that is connecting to your true North. That means tapping inward to who you truly are. That's why I say and feel that it's important to know who you are and have this true solid foundation as it was and is meant to be. We grow and we shift, but the foundation should not change unless it is helping you thrive.

The other part of being mind full is already having the space to be in true connection, in tune with source, which you should always be connected with and are. Let the fullness of that life-force flow through you to open your mind beyond its limits to cocreate at your highest capability. That means at your best. We are vessels. Let that both move you and raise your vibration to clearly commune with source directly. That happens inside of you. That should also be unique to your journey and who you are. Be guided with outside information, but be in touch with the real you and the source within.

Fully express yourself and who you are. I truly believe. At least for me, that is the beauty of real art. Yes, you might spark debate and everything else, but own your truth. It is the true masterpiece gifted by any Source/God (or any other name that goes by, to you individually, universally) you believe in. Let it flow through your voice, real and true. Mind Full. Mindful masterpiece you are. That I AM.

Creative Alchemy

Alchemy is the process of transmuting and changing or shifting energy. It is usually used to create something better when we put it into use for spiritual and/or creative alchemy. When we use alchemy for creative purposes, such as either past experiences or emotions or present experiences or emotions to create something beautiful, we uplift it. Transmuting the not-so-good into a healing and beautiful piece of art. Emotion, which is one of the many forms of energy, is an important form of energy, and in expressing it my way, I choose to create. We have the opportunity to change the vibration of energy for the better. By doing so, we heal and offer those who been through similar situations a way to connect and heal also. To not feel alone.

So, instead of holding it in or pretending we do not feel or experience things in life, we can, as creative artists, express our emotions and use art as a way to heal ourselves.

There is a book I read and loved that was very transformational in my own life. It's called *St Germaine on Alchemy* by Mark L. Prophet. It is basically about using your energy and emotions and shifting them into a higher transformative positive energy to empower others.

Well in layman terms but it is about something much deeper, much bigger. You will have to go read the book for yourself. We can use our emotions to turn them into beautiful art instead of using them for harm.

Our experiences can be expressed in our art. To do this, we must go within and feel and create from what we feel is true. True to who we are.

Intuitive creation

This is the bases true to my design that I must have as a foundation to create true. To create both multidimensionally and authentically according to me. I know we feed our minds through sight, touch, sound, and vibration. All of what is needed to create. We are all intuitive. It's just a matter of us tapping into our intuition. There are different forms of intuition, but I'll only speak of a few at the moment. Using these gifts to create are great tools to have.

Sight

What we see right in front of our eyes. Our eyes open or closed. Intuitive sight is being able to notice the everyday signs in an aware state of being. That can be written words written, or symbolic signs as well as other visual signs. Like what's directly in front of or what comes across your path throughout your day. Not only having the sight to see but also to know what they mean to you individually. It's good to know how what you see relates to you through your eyes and not another's eyes when you are learning to interpret. Yes, we all need a starting point, but honestly your soul knows. Try and start inward first. Outward can only validate or not. But true validation comes from within. Are the messages clear to you?

The easiest way I've learned to see is just to be. Stillness and/or music works for me. Sometimes it's me just being in motion. You find what works for you. Eyes open or closed, your intuitive eye can stay open should you choose.

Sound

We are all affected by sound. Shucks, the world was created through sound, so no wonder we are all affected by it. For me, it is important to make sure I sit with my creations and not only the obvious ones, my musical art, but also my painted art written works and other creations, to see how they internally in silence feel. That for me entails basically asking this, does it feel serene and balanced to me? Though I might not hear it, I will most definitely know the feel vibrationally, which in most cases is silent. Does it feel accurate and true to me?

The interesting thing about sound is that sometimes we cannot even hear certain sounds, pitches, etc. This is proven by animals having the ability to hear sounds and pitches and so on that our ears cannot.

Depending on the person and age of the person or how good their ears are, it is the same case. Sound, when it resonates with you, should not only sound good but feel good in this way.

Meaning that the sound brings you a sense of calm, comfort, relaxation, and even elation. I feel that even sounds not heard should invoke something within. Both the sound you cannot hear and the sound you can hear should invoke something.

Touch

How does your art feel, figuratively, physically, and intuitively? The intuitive gift of touch, that is, to be able to feel the energy of what you have created, is a great asset for any creator. What's that vibe? For those artists who paint, there are different textures they can you feel to the touch and also intuitively. Through your intuition you should be able to tell how something feels. Like, does it feel rough or soft? Smooth or rigid? What color does it remind you of? Do you have a sensation of warmth or coolness or nothing at all? Intuitively being able to tap into touch in its different aspects enables a whole other vibe and additional dimension to your creation. Plus, it just adds character. If you are creating music, how does that feel internally? This brings me to vibration.

Vibration

Again, vibration is how something feels internally. It's the usually unseen to the naked eye frequency of something and how it feels. Does it feel authentic to who you are? Does your creation empower you? If it does, great. If it doesn't, then change it. Does it flow easily? Sometimes it will flow easily and other times it will flow just at a bit of a different pace. Take that as a sign that something needs to be resolved within you or around you. Where are you at within yourself? What and who are you connecting with or sometimes that can be as simple as perspective. Other times, it could just be frame of mind or again that could be your environment and whether you yourself are in your true zone. I would suggest adjusting accordingly.

What do you feel emotionally about your work while creating it and at its finish? Do you feel at peace and have closure with those art pieces that are meant to be one-time pieces, unique? For those pieces that are meant to have additional work added, like a series, do you feel there is enough for more in the future, to continue on?

Conscious creation

Conscious creation is just another way of saying creating with intent in awareness. While there is both conscious and subconscious, my main focus is for you to be awake. Consciously knowing what you are creating. The goal is to have your subconscious in alignment with that as well. It doesn't need to be at 100%, but it does need to be at a high (what I consider close) alignment, at an energetic agreeance of both consciousnesses in allegiance to bringing forth the same thriving creation.

Conscious creation is so important because you create something with your *energy signature. You.* That is why I say to create authentically. True to who you are. You will create what you give life to in your consciousness. That's the way it's supposed to work anyway. There have been anomalies though. And I am one who believes, knows, that anything is possible when we move the limits we have placed on ourselves and either have allowed or not allowed others to place or transfer to us either consciously or subconsciously. How?

You've probably already read this or heard it before, but let me agree with the sentiments stated before. Outlets such as but not limited to TV, social media, radio, books, and other outlets seen and unseen that feed our mind through sight, touch, sound, and vibration. Please pay attention to. This means what you read, watch, and listen to. It's just as important as paying attention to what and who you surround yourself with physically and energetically. This is coming from a socially selective person in general who loves people.

Getting back to that conscious creation, at the end of the day, I feel we all want the best outcome available. Being aware of what you are creating, how you are creating, and even who you are creating with is all part of that equation. Be aware. Every step of the way. Every thought process you have. Let it flow. Just be aware, you intuitive creator.

What will you create?

Whatever it is, I hope it's fun, you, and genuine. Real and true to your vision. True to you. Don't limit yourself or allow limits on who you are or even on your creation. Do it with heart and integrity, and give it your all. Don't second guess it. Don't let anyone or anything stop you from creating your masterpiece.

Blank canvas or colorful one? Make it count! Let it shine; let it be number one in your eyes, the first.

Artistic tidbits about my authentic creations

Let's start with the spectrum wheel. While I have, since the start, used hues vibrationally and figuratively, such as reds and greens, I have been consistent with the use of several other colors. Those colors I have not changed throughout the years because primordially they are true to who I am in any given creative vibration. Even yet, true to my design my colors and hues used do not necessarily mean the same thing you were taught. It might be close if it incorporates rising and correctly aligning the vibration, sound, people and vessels multidimensionally. These colors or hues are shades of blue, yellow/Gold, shades of purple (including magenta, which has a kiss of pink), pastel pink (which incorporates white and pink together), shades of white (such as cream, which is a mixture of beige and white), and lastly, jumping back into red. When I use this color, it is firm and passionate.

Colors, like vibrational sound, are very important to me for how I, the cocreator, am impacted physically, mentally, and emotionally. Does it heal me or does it harm me? My true "yeses" are those creations that impact me in a way to both heal and grow, complete and whole. Something I can feel just by throwing on a pair of headphones and being still.

Vibrational sounds are tonal sounds that I use in my music. Some of these are AU, EL, OO, and EE. They are subtle most times but play a very important role in my music. Whether it's as a lead vocal or background vocal, these sounds/tonal sounds are true to my energetic signature when used correctly.

While I'd love to give you more information on what these tones mean and can do vibrationally in the physical and spiritual body, but I'd like for you to do your own research. There are primordial uses for these tones in certain cultures beyond the basic cool sounds and additions they bring to any song. I hope what you find helps you to grow as a conscious artist and person. That you can use them to empower your own path or even find more tonal sounds that resonate with your true you. Your soul.

The vibe and feel of my current music, regardless of any genre it would be placed in, is chill, ambient with a mix of dance electronica and Soul. You should feel a blanket of love, healing, and just being focused in the moment from the music. I continue to push for vulnerability in my sound. In truth, my sound is unmatched and incomparable. At least, not with those who have the sight and hearing tuned to true authenticity. I incorporate passion, even if it is gentle, and, yes, sometime even with a more felt presence and force so that the intention is made clear.

What are the intentions and vibes for your own creations in truth?

These are just extra tidbits of me being and creating AUTHENTIC from day one as an artist true to my design. Everyone has their way. Mine is my own with an amazing cocreator and in all acceptance of who I AM, unique to thrive. To live. To flourish. To Love. To be true to who I AM.

Latest Ep releases

Latest Ep releases since The Last booklet I've released some music both available to streaming an a couple not available for streaming that can only be found at reverbnation.com/SheisL1.

I will only discuss the latest two EP Release titled More Life and Love Me Right both from last quarter of 2022.

More Life Ep is more of a dance ambiance mixed with a little stellar. Created for a lounge vibe in sound and in vibration.

Something Real is just saying we all not only need but deserve something real. That's real as in the things, people and so on that help us thrive as individuals and as Hu-Manity.

More Life is about breathing more good life into this world and the ones, things we love.

Call Me is intuitively speaking to my real people saying call me if you need me and I'll be there in the way I as best as I can on a dessert night. Dessert is a sacred place.

Desert Night As simple as I can put it without too much detail is it's about a dessert Knight (not what will probably be assumed) and on a desert night . I'm stating that it was his eye and eyes that lite up the night, not the stars.

Stellaric MelloShe is an instrumental with two different sounds with drum then transitioning over to stellar in instrumental.

FrequenShe EL has tonal of a couple of those notes I wrote about above combined with more of a meditative sound in ambience for total relaxation and sound healing.

Next to release was Love Me Right. This 5 track EP was released in December of 2022.My version of soul music and electronic mixed together created for the eclectic and experimental in sound listening pallets. True to SheisL1 Design.

Love Me Right

This first track Love Me Right, is about calling in a love true to come into my life and love me like I've never been loved. That is raw, sweet, loyal, supportive and all the other qualities I've learned I cannot compromise on. Nor should anyone. With that said and knowing that I am intuitive it is meant as an intuitive calling for the true manifestation of this man.

Dream A Reality was written to say let's make the wheel of SheisL1 correct and a reality to thrive unlike what I have seen and not at all a part of Patrice Hickombottom's my true design.

Boomerang is about the boomerang and power of real love. So it is not a boomerang of harm but instead a boomerang to spread more real life and love.

Should Have Seen was written about those toxic playboy connections. The playboys that have a real love available and misuse mistreat and who are never satisfied. Their system is based on superficial, egotistical, fake love and manipulations.

Deserve was a very important one for me to get out. My way of expressing my disgust of a group beings, participants misusing the mind, the access of my vessel while mistreating and stealing from me as an unique artist, person and my real life for their "persona" and profit against my wheel . As an artist I hope you do not have to experience this. I spoke some about it earlier and even in my previous booklets about the misuse of organizations and known in the public eye artists using intellectual mind and other ideas based off of someone who is not as known in the public eye and without permission, without agreement and without contract signed in ink.

Quotes for life, love, and music

All of these quotes are my original quotes. I hope they add a sense of upliftment and optimism to your day and your journey.

Everyone's interpretation of art is something different and based off of their own beliefs. Beautiful art makes people feel, connect, and think.

If art on a canvas has the power to move, imagine what a true voice can do. Sound.

If it calls you to your true home, that is the way. If it pulls you away, let it stray.

No voice is as important as your own inner voice. Your voice to feed your body, heart, soul, and mind.

It should move you, empower you, and shift you forward in your true greatness. "It" being anything from art, life, or people.

Who are you doing it for and why?

Does it uplift and empower you though?

A temporary win for a temporary win or a lifelong win for life? Thrive beyond.

Does it balance in action and energy? In mind and grounded reality?

Is that energy in a harmonious two-way flow or just one way?

What can you materially take away from that creation? What can you spiritually take away from it?

What kind of impression did your art leave on you as the artist first? What impression did it leave on the person, viewing, listening, or touching and reading your art?

Everything we see in art leaves some type of mark in our experience. Was it what you set out to do?

We are always creating and choosing. While choosing ourselves, we can also help others, but don't take their stories as your own. Your greatness was already created in you before your birth. Own it, don't waste it.

Live for you while walking with others as a community who share best interests for you and you for them. This creates harmony of minds not friction. This is not science. This is real life.

There is never and I say never an excuse excusable to dishonor the ones who honored you true, real. There is forgiveness and grace that is found on walking separate paths with the ones you trust. Those who honor themselves so much that they either honor you or they have the dignity to not pretend.

What it is perceived to be truth depends on where you are standing and viewing from. But the truth won't change the real truth regardless of perception.

Your art should have your true energy signature unique to you and no other artist, unless you are collaborating with them. The beauty of your uniqueness is who you were born as and who you were meant to be without regrets, just growth.

We don't have to see eye to eye, but we do need to be open to what another's point of view can bring. We do need to have the best intentions for one another. We do need to choose one another. It's a two-way street not one but as ONE.

Perfect was never the goal unless it was perfect to the creator which is beautifully imperfect in itself. Being true is. Being true to who you are should be the goal.

Is profound art, art if it doesn't make you question something? Such as life, you, or your journey? Or if it doesn't have you seeing through different perspectives?

They say it's all relative. Just make sure it's relative to who you are, and who you choose to be and become. Relative to your highest.

Each project you choose to take on, I feel not only should you grow in it but it is imperative that you grow from project to project. Notice your transformations and view. How they have changed or stayed the same, and how have you as a person done the same?

There are a billions eyes in this world. So imagine all the perspectives. None, not one, is as important as what and how you see yourself and your projects through your eye and eyes. Not if you are looking for inward, soulful fulfillment.

Your mind is your computer. Your heart is your battery. Your body is your house/temple. How will you choose to nourish, love, and grow all of these so that they successfully work together in harmony? This is your artistic trinity. The soul is all-encompassing with all the knowledge you need to get things done for life, for art, for you.

What part of yourself will you choose to create from: your mind, your heart, your gut/intuition, your soul, or all?

Books by Leigh Hickombottom, also known as SheisL1

These titles are available under the name Leigh Hickombottom:

Logistics of Leanness

Logistics of Leanness Defined

7 Tools That Transform

And Still I Smile

These titles are available under the name SheisL1:

The Music

The Music Loveology X Integrity

Table of Contents

The Music:

Authenticity Code

SheisL 1

This is my way of helping to guide others like me to be authentic and know being different, weird and owning your gifts is something to be celebrated every day. Some tools from my journey of having to do it almost ALL on my own without an entourage of people doing it for me and protecting the voice, the wheel. Don't let people steal who you are in real life for their financial gain to look good in public. Unknown artists protect and defend your works of art and who you are. There is something such as authentic creators who give credit whether they are in the public eye or not. It's about respecting other artist's minds, gifts and talents. I have seen unknown creative intellectual minds be used, stolen and misused by artists in the public eye who had the opportunity to correct their wrongs and still chose to pull off unknown true creative minds ideas, looks etc. These experiences helped to inspire this third booklet. You are enough.

With Love and support for the unique, different and choosing to grow together ones (artists).~SheisL1

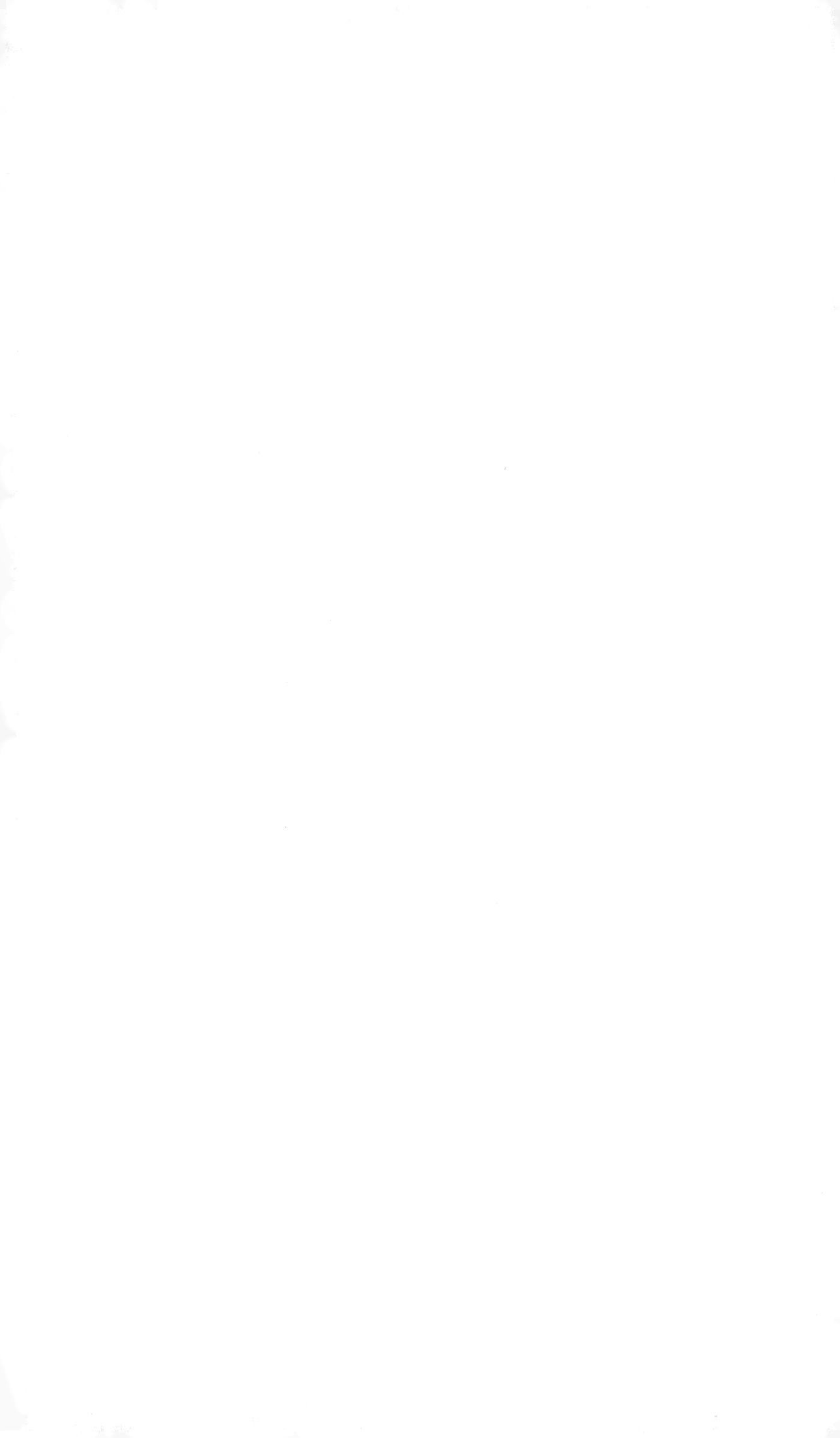

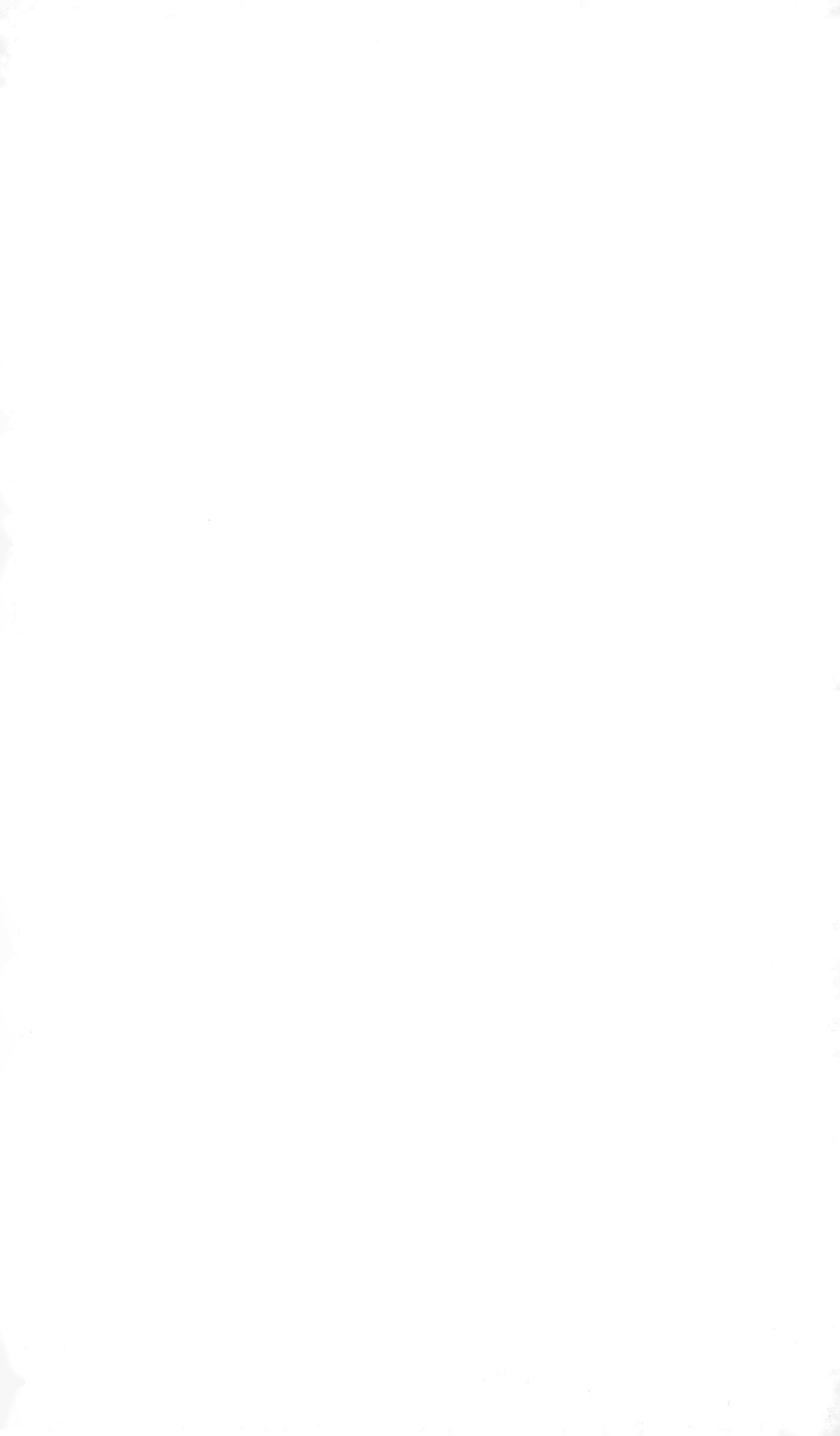

www.ingramcontent.com/pod-product-compliance
Lightning Source LLC
LaVergne TN
LVHW010943110826
845149LV00013B/2738

* 9 7 8 0 9 9 1 4 5 2 9 6 5 *